WEAVING THREADS OF GOLD

WEAVING THREADS OF GOLD

JUDY MAID

WEAVING THREADS OF GOLD

A 31-Day Devotional of Encountering Hope in Unexpected Places

Copyright © 2023 Judy Maid. All rights reserved.
Contact: judymaid@yahoo.com

No part of this publication may be reproduced, distributed, or transmitted in any form or by any means, including photocopying, recording, or other electronic or mechanical methods, without the prior written permission of the publisher, except in the case of brief quotations embodied in critical reviews and certain other noncommercial uses permitted by copyright law.

Cover Design and Formatting by Meg Delagrange

All scripture references are from the New American Standard Bible and the New Living Translation

First edition, 2023

*To my daughters,
who are the golden threads
in the tapestry of my life.*

Introduction

For as long as I can remember, writing has always been something I have been passionate about. Whether it's writing about my personal journey, observations from nature, or everyday events, I always find allegories that help me paint word pictures of the situation. Just like an artist with a paintbrush, I feel this is my creative outlet, and it brings me great satisfaction.

My hope is the pictures I paint and the words I write will help you continue on your path and reach your full potential. I have always loved to help people find vision for their life, and I believe, no matter how dark the day, with God's help and strength, we can climb any mountain and reach our summit.

A Note to You

DEAR READER, I am delighted you have chosen to read my devotional. May the words and allegories I have shared bring refreshment to your soul and help you to embrace all God has made you to be. My prayer is that you would fulfill the purposes God planned for you long before you were born. I hope each reflective question will speak to you and help you get in touch with yourself in a meaningful way.

If this devotional has breathed hope into your heart, then I have accomplished my mission. I would love to hear from you with any comments, questions, or feedback you may have. May these writings help you to weave your threads of gold, creating your own beautiful tapestry.

I can be reached at judymaid@yahoo.com

DAY ONE

The Tapestry

ARE THERE TIMES in your journey when nothing in your life seems to make sense? You have questions that go unanswered, and you end up feeling lost and confused?

As the Scripture says, *"Hope deferred makes the heart sick, but desire fulfilled is a tree of life." Proverbs 13:12*

It is during times such as these we need to believe God is doing a deeper work despite the silence and turmoil we find ourselves in. It is a time where we walk by faith and not by sight. *(2 Corinthians 5:7)*

I personally have experienced dark times like the ones I just described when the silence of God was deafening. I became disheartened and, at times, without hope.

During one particular time, a dear friend shared a story about a tapestry with me. When I looked at the underside of this work of art, all I could see were threads going every which way. Some of the threads were unraveling and some look frayed. There were an array of colors, such as yellow, red, blue, green, and even threads of gold and silver. The colors were beautiful, but they had no harmony. If you looked at it, you would be tempted to discard it.

And then, I turned the tapestry over, and right before my eyes was a magnificent work of art. It was filled with such beauty that it almost took my breath away. What specifically made it so stunning was the black background that accented the beautiful colors and made it stand out and look glorious!

So it is in our life. In the dark and most silent times, God is creating a masterpiece. He organizes all the colors into a beautiful landscape of your life.

Please remember, dear reader, God is the craftsman creating your own exquisite tapestry with everything in its proper place.

My prayer for you is that through this allegory, your vision for your future will inspire you as you trust in the beautiful outcome that will come to pass.

REFLECTION

Which side of the tapestry are you seeing now?

_____
_____
_____
_____
_____
_____

Was there a time when you saw the beautiful side of the tapestry? If so, what was it?

_____
_____
_____
_____
_____
_____

Yet God has made everything beautiful for its own time. He has planted eternity in the human heart, but even so, people cannot see the whole scope of God's work from beginning to end.

ECCLESIASTES 3:11

DAY TWO

Discover Your True Identity

IDENTITY THEFT is a serious problem affecting millions of people each year. It can be a confusing and frustrating experience to have your personal identity stolen or compromised. But as I thought about the concept of identity theft, I realized there is another kind of identity theft we can all fall victim to: the theft of our true identity in Christ.

So often, we allow ourselves to be influenced by the lies and distortions the enemy of our soul wants us to believe about ourselves. We may believe we are not good enough, or we will never measure up, or we are not worthy, or God doesn't care about us, or we are a failure. These lies can steal away the identity God has given us and leave us feeling lost and confused.

But the good news is we have a savior who came to give us life and life to the full. Jesus said, "The thief comes to steal, kill, and destroy, but I have come that they may have life and have it to the fullest" *(John 10:10)*. He wants you to experience the fullness of life which comes from knowing and living out your true identity in Him.

So how can you discover your true identity in Christ and overcome the lies you may have believed about yourself? It starts by listening to the voice of truth and meditating on what God says about you. Open the Bible to discover who God says you are and then choose to believe it.

Here are some truths from the Word of God which will help you reclaim your identity in Christ:

"You are loved with an everlasting love."
- *Jeremiah 31:3*
"You are worthy." - *1 Timothy 1:15*
"You are a royal priesthood." - *1 Peter 2:9*
"You are chosen." - *1 Peter 2:4*
"You are my child." - *Romans 8:14-17*
"You are an overcomer and victorious."
- *Romans 8:37*
"You are forgiven." - *Colossians 1:14*
"Nothing or no one will ever separate you from my love." - *Romans 8:38-39*

As you meditate on these truths and allow them to sink deep into your heart, soul, and mind, your identity in Christ can never be taken away from you. I pray your eyes will be opened to see all that God says about you and you will experience the pure love that He has for you.

REFLECTION

What lies do you tend to believe about yourself?

_____
_____
_____
_____
_____
_____
_____

What truths can you replace them with?

_____
_____
_____
_____
_____
_____
_____

He predestined us to adoption as sons and daughters through Jesus Christ to Himself, according to the good pleasure of His will.

EPHESIANS 1:5

DAY THREE

Be Yourself

"*Allow me to be who I am through you.*" I heard those words one cold winter evening while driving home from work. In my heart, I was speaking to the Lord about what His will and plans were for me in the New Year ahead.

When I heard the Lord speaking to me, I felt like a lightning bolt hit me! I was expecting to hear something like *"work with the homeless, go on a mission trip, or serve in some capacity in the church."* The words were burning in my soul, and as I meditated, I realized I was not true to who God made me be. I was going in different directions, trying to be somebody else and doing things that weren't working. How could God use me if I wasn't living a genuine and sincere life and allowing Him to reign in my life through my uniqueness?

Living a life through how God made us in our uniqueness is truly the only way we can impact those around us and be a positive difference in this world. I looked around me at the unique ways God expresses Himself through nature. An elephant isn't supposed to run like a cheetah, a dog is not meant to purr like a kitten, and a sunflower is not meant to be fragrant like the lilac bush. If one is an introvert, he doesn't have to be the life of the party, and if God made me express myself through music, I shouldn't be behind a desk, crunching numbers.

These examples brought me divine relief and a peace I hadn't experienced in a long time. I was free to be me, and as I celebrated, the Lord directed me on how I could impact my world through my unique personality, experiences, and spiritual gifts that He creatively made me have.

How about you? Are you celebrating who God made you to be? Or have you lost vision of who you are and fallen into the trap of trying to be someone else? Allowing God to be who He is through us is one of the most freeing and exhilarating experiences we can have as we journey through this life.

REFLECTION

What does an authentic life look like for you?

_____
_____
_____
_____
_____
_____
_____

What would happen if you showed up as you truly are?

_____
_____
_____
_____
_____
_____
_____

*There are different kinds of gifts, but the same
Spirit distributes them.*

1 CORINTHIANS 12:4

DAY FOUR

Just a Little Light

I'VE BEEN THINKING and meditating on the word 'HOPE.' Hope brings a sense of expectation and desire for a certain thing to happen.

To me, hope is like a candle burning in a dark room. It brings enough light for us to see, but we expect the lights to eventually be more than just a little light and make the room brighter.

Hope gives us strength when we are weak and vision for what has not transpired in our lives yet. I love the scripture in Romans 15:13, which says, *"Now may the God of hope fill you with all joy and peace in believing, that you may abound in hope by the power of the Holy Spirit."*

Abound is a word that means providing a plentiful supply or quantity. The Lord never gives anything little, but He gives us in abundance in our time of need.

Never before have we had more of a need for hope to abound in our lives and the world. Romans 5:5 says, *"and hope does not disappoint because the love of God has been poured out within our hearts through the Holy Spirit who was given to us."*

Dear friend, what do you hope and pray for? Whatever it may be, make it known to God and trust the Lord will not disappoint you, and He will fill you with His love through the power of the Holy Spirit.

REFLECTION

How can you cultivate hope in your life?

_____
_____
_____
_____
_____
_____
_____

What is something that makes you feel hopeful right now?

_____
_____
_____
_____
_____
_____
_____

And hope does not put us to shame, because God's love has been poured out into our hearts through the Holy Spirit, who has been given to us.

ROMANS 5:5

DAY FIVE

Undeserved Favor

I GREW UP IN AN EXTREMELY strict church, otherwise known as *legalistic*. Because I was always obedient to the rules, this came very easily to me. The issue was, even though I was striving so hard to obey the rules, I never felt like it was enough. I was in a performance-based religion, which eventually held me in bondage. I felt shame and guilt when I fell short of what I thought my performance should have been. The nagging feelings would not disappear until a friend told me about grace.

The word *'grace'* seemed so foreign to me until I read the scripture that awakened my soul. Ephesians 2:8 and 9, *"For by grace you have been saved by faith and that not of yourselves, it is a gift of God not of works, lest any man boast."*

Grace means undeserved favor. God revealed to me I no longer had to strive and perform to be acknowledged by people, rather I need to trust and please Him, the Almighty Father. What a gift that was to me! It brought Divine relief to my heart. To realize I no longer had to work to please people but instead have faith in the sacrifice Jesus made on the cross. This scripture confirmed what I was learning in Galatians 2:16, *"A man is not justified by the works of the law, but through faith in Christ Jesus."*

The life I live now is led by a grace which sets me free. Now when I do things that are good, right, and pleasing to God, it is by His grace, not my works.

Someone once told me religion is spelled **DO** and having a connection with God is spelled

DONE. I am no more doing but instead focusing on building my connection with the Lord.

I pray that your true heart will see and experience the power of a personal relationship with Jesus.

"If the son shall set you free, you are free indeed." Freedom feels so good to experience!

REFLECTION

Have you had a time in your life when grace freed you from the shackles of legalism?

_____
_____
_____
_____
_____
_____

Is it difficult to receive God's Grace when you fall short of living the life He has for you?

_____
_____
_____
_____
_____
_____

For by grace you have been saved through faith; it is the gift of God; not as a result of works, so that no man can boast.

EPHESIANS 2:8-9

DAY SIX

No Looking Back

ONE DAY, I read a quote that caught my attention: "there's a reason the rearview mirror is so small, and the windshield is so big. Where you're headed is so much more important than what you left behind."

How often do we look back and ask ourselves questions such as *"What would my life look like if I could change that?" "Why was my past so painful?"* These questions can be good for reflection so we can learn from the past. The problem comes when we remain stuck in the past because we are left with feelings of shame, regret, remorse, and sadness.

These feelings become like shackles around our feet and prevent us from experiencing new beginnings and embracing more blessings.

I remember my early childhood when I hoped and wished things could have been different. At the time, I was worried and full of questions that needed answers. I wondered, *"What if I received more attention from my parents, "What if I took school more seriously?" "What if I had teachers who encouraged me to do my best in school?" "What would my life look like if I didn't make that decision?"* Too many *'What if'* questions kept me lost in my thoughts. I was stuck. I realized I wasn't living in the present, savoring all the beautiful people and things that the present time had given me.

Hebrews 12:1 reminds us to *"lay aside every encumbrance and the sin which so easily entangles us, and let us run with endurance the race that is set before us, placing our trust in Jesus."*

Can you imagine a runner with shackles on his feet trying to run his race? He wouldn't get very far.

So it is with our race of life if we continue to run and hold on to the past. We will remain stuck and not experience the new beginnings that the Lord has prepared for us.

Let today be the day you leave your shackles at the feet of Jesus and be free to run without any encumbrances holding you back. As the saying goes, "When you let your past decide your present, you have destroyed your future." Trust in Jesus and move forward with hope and purpose.

REFLECTION

What is holding you back from letting go of the past?

_____
_____
_____
_____
_____
_____

What steps can you take today to free yourself from the past?

_____
_____
_____
_____
_____
_____

Brothers, I do not count myself to have attained, but one thing I do, forgetting those things which are behind and reaching forward to those things which are ahead. I press towards the goal to the prize of the high calling of God in Christ Jesus.

PHILIPPIANS 3:13-14

DAY SEVEN

New Glory Is in the Works

WINTER HAD ARRIVED in full force. Except for the snow drifts that continue to increase, there was no trace of anything growing. The days were becoming shorter, and the sun was hiding behind clouds. Looking at it with my physical eyes, it showed no trace of life anywhere.

What we typically fail to recognize during the colder months is that they are the most productive time of year. The earth is hard at work preparing for the splendor of spring, beautiful flowers, green pastures, blossoming trees, cascading waterfalls, and much more.

Never has the winter of my soul felt darker than that one, as the snow drifts slowly grew around my weary soul. It was a time when hope was nowhere to be found, and God's presence seemed even harder to find. There were no signs of life or God working, or so it seemed.

On one of my darker days, I felt the Lord opening my eyes to what was really going on for the first time. The Lord gave me a revelation of the work He does in winter to produce the glory of spring, and He was doing it in my soul. The Lord was preparing me for fulfilling greater depths of His purposes for my life. For the first time, I could embrace the night of my soul because I had renewed hope and vision of all God was preparing me for.

The imaginary snow drifts which held my soul captive began to melt as my hope and vision came alive. I think of the Proverbs verse that says people faint without vision. And also, *"Hope deferred makes the heart sick, but desire fulfilled is a tree of life."* The tree of life in my soul was budding, and I could hardly wait to see what fruit would be displayed.

Today I pray your eyes will be opened to the work God is doing in your life, even during the darkest and coldest times. I pray you trust God for his plans for your future and receive a vision for all God is preparing you for.

I pray that the eyes of your heart may be enlightened in order that you may know the hope to which he has called you, the riches of his glorious inheritance in his holy people.

EPHESIANS 1:18

REFLECTION

What did you do when you lost vision for what God was doing in your life?

How did you regain hope for your future?

DAY EIGHT

The Beauty of Freedom

ON THE FOURTH OF JULY, I witnessed a stunning fireworks show. I was overwhelmed by the vivid colors and tremendous booms. What an apt expression of our forefathers' vision. They stated in the Declaration of Independence that their nation would never surrender to kings or dictators. They made the courageous choice to declare independence from the tyranny of other nations and governments.

Freedom. I've been considering the beauty of its promise. You are free to be who you aspire to be. But just as our founding fathers fought for our freedom, we, too, must fight for our own freedom.

So many ways interfere with the flow of our personal freedom. We can become our worst enemies as we start to believe the many lies that come into our minds. Lies such as *"I'm not enough," "I'll never measure up," "I'm not smart enough, good enough, pretty enough,"* and the list goes on.

Jesus said in John 8:32, *"You will know the truth and the truth will make you free."* Now that's a powerful promise worth looking into. And what are the truths He is talking about? He tells us we are loved unconditionally; we are enough because of His Spirit dwelling in us; we do not need to work for His love and acceptance; we can do all things because of the strength He gives us. These are just a few of the many powerful promises that will release us from the power of the enemy.

In order for that to happen, we need to make our own personal declaration, declaring we will no longer subject ourselves to the lies and distortions that have held us captive.

America's freedoms didn't come without sacrifice

or a fight. And so it is for us. We must fight and stand against the lies and enemies who would hold us back.

So, my friend, I pray as you experience your breakthroughs in freedom, the beauty and power from within will far exceed the fireworks of this year's Fourth. May you break free from the chains that have shackled your heart and mind.

REFLECTION

What's holding you back from living a freedom-filled life?

_____
_____
_____
_____
_____
_____
_____

Write a declaration about your personal freedom today:

_____
_____
_____
_____
_____
_____
_____

It was for freedom that Christ set us free; therefore keep standing firm and do not be subject again to a yoke of slavery.

GALATIANS 5:1

DAY NINE

Take Refuge in His Love

RECENTLY I SPENT some time in Florida after hurricane Ian hit. The devastation I witnessed was beyond my comprehension. Boats layered on top of one another, trees torn apart, homes completely destroyed, and mountains of sand piled higher than the buildings that were still standing. My heart was broken. I had to turn back because it was too much to take in.

Once I was home, I could not help but reflect on how this impacted countless people. One day they're sitting on the balcony, taking in the beauty of the ocean, listening to birds singing, and feeling a gentle breeze on their face, and suddenly they're told they have to evacuate. I can't imagine what thoughts they had as they left everything they possessed.

We all have experienced our personal hurricanes in one way or another—death of our loved ones, divorce, loss of a job, or all our possessions. But God promises us in Romans 8:35-37, *"What shall separate us from the love of Christ? Shall tribulation, or distress or persecution or famine, or nakedness or peril or sword or (hurricanes) In all these things we are more than conquerors through Him who loved us."*

Catastrophic times can take away all our earthly possessions. It can crush our spirit and make us feel hopeless. But with God's help, we can rise above the ashes and find hope and restoration. These tough times will test us to the depths of our souls.

When everything is destroyed and taken away, we come to terms with what is most important, our relationship with a loving God and those who are dear to us.

No matter what has happened to you, may you take refuge in God's protection and find His loving arms wrapped around you, bringing you peace and hope.

REFLECTION

Write about a difficult experience that ultimately brought unexpected blessings to your life:

_____
_____
_____
_____
_____
_____
_____
_____

Did you reach out for help during that time? Why or how?

_____
_____
_____
_____
_____

And we know that all things work together for good to those who love God, to those who are called according to His purpose.

ROMANS 8:28

DAY TEN

The Tongue Can Break a Heart

HAVE YOU EVER stopped to think about the impact of your words? I read a quote the other day that caught my attention, "The tongue has no bones, but it is strong enough to break a heart, so be careful with your words."

That got me thinking about my third grade teacher Mrs. Becker who obviously didn't like me. There was an occasion when she made me stand up in front of the class and had the other students tell me what they didn't like about me.

The words spoken crushed my spirit, and I felt very humiliated. Many years later, I still remember how that impacted me, but her words and the words of the other students would not have the final say!

On the other side of that story was my fourth-grade teacher, Miss Jason. I feel like crying when I think of her and the impact her encouragement and recommendations had on me. She always had kind words for me and made extra efforts to make me feel special. When I was around her a sense of comfort and peace filled my heart.

Obviously, the difference in these two situations affected me in very different ways. Proverbs 18:21 speaks about the power that our words can have on people. *"Death and life are in the power of the tongue and those who love it will eat its fruit."* One brought death to my soul and the other brought life and encouragement.

Proverbs 16:24 really summarizes it well. *"Pleasant words are a honeycomb sweet to the soul and healing to the bones."*

Wherever you are and whomever you're with, take the time to think about the impact of your words. You can put life into the words you speak, just as Miss Jason did for me. Or death and shame, as Ms. Becker tried to do to me. I pray by God's Grace, you will speak words of life that can turn someone's life around.

REFLECTION

Who in your life spoke words of life to you and how did that impact you?

_____
_____
_____
_____
_____
_____
_____
_____

Is there someone in your life today you can speak words of life to?

_____
_____
_____
_____
_____

A gentle tongue is a tree of life,
but perversion in it crushes the spirit.

PROVERBS 15:4

DAY ELEVEN

Forgiveness

SOMETIMES WE FEEL weighed down by extra baggage and we're not sure where it's coming from. It could be something simple like not getting enough sleep, a poor diet, not exercising enough, or dehydration. These things are easy to identify and fix if we take a step back and take care of our physical selves.

Other times, it's not so easy. Disappointments, hurts, betrayal, misunderstandings, etc., can weigh heavily on our hearts and it's harder to let go. It's easy to become bitter or hold onto grudges when we feel wounded by someone we care about. As the saying goes, "Unforgiveness is like drinking poison and expecting someone else to die."

Jesus has a lot to say about forgiveness and its power. Matthew 6:14 says, *"For if you forgive other people when they sin against you, your heavenly Father will also forgive you."* Colossians 3:13 adds, *"Bear with each other and forgive one another if any of you has a grievance against someone. Forgive as the Lord forgave you."*

Forgiveness is often a process and doesn't happen overnight. But it always begins with a choice. Just like we might not always want to exercise, we make a choice to do so because we know it will make us feel and look better. The same is true with forgiveness. We might not always want to let go of our hurts, but when we choose to forgive, we feel better physically, emotionally, and most importantly, spiritually. We feel lighter, and more at peace, and we feel more of the Lord's presence.

I don't want to minimize the deep pain and wounds that you may have. When we invite God into those places, He can bring healing to our hearts. (Malachi 4:2), *"But to you who revere my name, the sun of righteousness will rise with healing in its wings. And you will go free, leaping with joy like calves let out in the pasture."* To be free from the prison of our hurts brings true and lasting freedom. I pray you will experience that freedom today.

REFLECTION

If you're ready to begin the process of forgiveness, here are some questions to consider:

Is there anything that causes you to hold onto your deep hurts?

_____

_____

_____

_____

_____

_____

_____

_____

What can you do to start the process of forgiveness?

_____
_____
_____
_____
_____
_____
_____
_____

How might you feel after you've forgiven someone?

_____
_____
_____
_____
_____

> *Then Peter came up and said to Him, "Lord, how many times shall my brother sin against me and I still forgive him? Up to seven times?" Jesus said to him, "I do not say to you, up to seven times, but up to seventy-seven times.*
>
> MATTHEW 18:22

DAY TWELVE

Flowers in the Desert

I'VE BEEN THINKING and meditating lately on how flowers thrive in the desert. The desert is often seen as a barren and inhospitable place, but it is in these dry and seemingly lifeless lands where some of the most beautiful and vibrant flowers thrive.

This got me thinking about how the desert can serve as a metaphor for our lives. Sometimes, our souls feel parched and life is complicated. But even in these difficult times, God is at work, bringing forth beautiful flowers in the form of His loving presence, the love of others, daily grace and mercy, His peace, and the living water found in His Word.

As we journey through our own personal deserts, it's important to remember God sees us in our suffering and uses it to comfort others. II Corinthians tells us we can comfort those in affliction with the same comfort we received from God. And in Isaiah 43:18-20, we are reminded not to dwell on the past, but to look forward to the new things God will do.

So if you're feeling weary on your journey and find yourself in a desert, know that God is with you and will sustain you. And He will use your struggles to bring about a greater comeback. Trust in Him and have hope for the future as you enter your personal Promised Land.

Therefore they will come and sing aloud on the height of Zion, streaming to the goodness of the Lord – for wheat, for wine, for oil, for the young of the flock and the herd; and their soul will be like a watered garden, and they will never be weary.

JEREMIAH 31:12

REFLECTION

In what ways can you seek the "goodness of the Lord" in your own life?

_____

_____

_____

_____

_____

_____

_____

_____

Was there a time when flowers showed up in your desert? If so, what were they?

_____

_____

_____

_____

_____

_____

_____

DAY THIRTEEN

Nourish the Soil of Your Heart

I USED TO LOVE GARDENING when I lived in Illinois. The soil was dark and rich, and anything I planted seemed to grow quickly and beautifully. But when I moved to Colorado, the soil was very different. It was thick, hard, and clay-like, and no matter how much time and money I spent trying to replicate the soil I had in Illinois, it just didn't work.

This experience got me thinking about the soil of our hearts and what is being planted and taking root there. Jesus spoke about the various soils and compared them to the seeds sown on them. There were rocky soils, soils with no roots, soils with thorns, and finally, good soil. *(See Matthew 13:18-23)*

So how do we maintain the soil of our hearts like good, rich soil? By nourishing it with water and fertilizer. We take in the water of God's Word, and our souls are deeply nourished. We fertilize through fellowship with one another. And we weed by addressing our sins and shortcomings.

I pray the soil of your heart would be rich and fertile, allowing the fruit of the spirit to flourish in your life. I pray the Holy Spirit would help you nourish your heart with God's Word and fellowship with others.

REFLECTION

How can you keep the soil of your heart soft?

_____
_____
_____
_____
_____
_____
_____

What discipline can you take to have good, rich soil in your heart?

_____
_____
_____
_____
_____
_____

Watch over your heart with all diligence,
for from it flow the springs of life.

PROVERBS 4:23

DAY FOURTEEN

Facing a Mountain

SOMETIMES IN OUR LIVES, we may experience overwhelming challenges that seem difficult to overcome. One of these occurred when I went to California to learn how to snow ski. Fear gripped me when I looked at the mountains, and I didn't pass the class because I kept falling. I was so agitated and felt defeated. I was facing a mountain that had paralyzed me with fear.

But as I took a lunch break, the Lord spoke to me through two Scriptures: *"Perfect love casts out all fear"* and *"I can do all things through Christ who gives me strength."*

As I prayed these Scriptures, my fear turned into faith and the burden was lifted. I returned to the mountain with confidence and felt like a ballerina on skis. It was exhilarating!

When we imagine our problems to be greater than God, we stumble and lose sight of what He alone can do, no matter how big the mountain we are confronting. Ephesians 3:20-21 reminds us He is able to do *"exceedingly abundantly above all that we ask or think, according to the power that works in us."*

I realized I was seeing that mountain through a lens of doubt and fear. We need to change the filter of what we are thinking about and bring the lens of truth to our circumstances. It is then and only then we will find no mountain too high, no valley too low, where God comes on the scene and intervenes on our behalf. Let us turn whatever is heavy on our hearts to His throne of Grace so He can show up in a powerful way.

REFLECTION

If you look deep enough, what is it you are afraid of?

_____
_____
_____
_____
_____
_____
_____

How can you, with God's help, overcome some of your fears?

_____
_____
_____
_____
_____
_____

Fear not, for I am with you, Be not dismayed, for I am your God, I will strengthen you, yes I will help you, I will uphold you with my righteous right hand.

ISAIAH 41:10

DAY FIFTEEN

A State of Gratitude

I ONCE HEARD IT SAID, "Living in a state of gratitude is the gateway to grace." How often do we think, *"I'll be happy when such and such happens."* *"I would be happy if only that didn't happen to me."* When our minds go in such directions, we can be sure of one thing. Happiness for the present time, will not be found. Someone else once said, "One's happiness does not depend on what happens to that person." Joy comes from within, regardless of our circumstances.

There was a time when I realized my "attitude of gratitude" was way off. So, I decided to start a gratitude journal. I would end my day writing down at least five things I was grateful for. Even when I had a bad day and everything seemed to go wrong, I still found there were so many things I could be grateful for. The shelter of my home, the food I ate that day, the sunset I witnessed, friends and family surrounding me. No matter what, there was always something to be grateful for.

This discipline changed the course of my life, and I began to experience the abundant joy I never had before. It gave me a greater awareness of all the lovely and beautiful gifts that were right before me. Psalm 105:1 reminds us to, *"give thanks to the Lord, for He is good, His loving-kindness is everlasting."* 1 Thessalonians 5:18 says, *"In all things give thanks for this is the will of God for you in Christ Jesus."*

I pray the joy from gratitude will set you on a new path and your happiness will not be mistaken for what God's happiness alone can provide. I'll end with this quote which I thought brought home the power of our attitude. "A negative attitude is like a flat tire, you won't get anywhere until you change it." Choose to focus on the good things in your life and let gratitude lead you to a place of grace and joy.

Rejoice always, pray without ceasing, in everything give thanks; for this is the will of God for you in Christ Jesus.

I THESSALONIANS 5:16-18

REFLECTION

How can you practice an attitude of gratitude even in the face of difficult times?

_____

_____

_____

_____

_____

_____

List five things you are grateful for:

_____

_____

_____

_____

_____

_____

_____

_____

_____

_____

DAY SIXTEEN

What Are You Thinking About?

DO YOU EVER take a moment to examine the thoughts in your heart? What has been taking up the most space in your heart and mind? Every idea we have has a powerful influence on the path we choose in life. Proverbs 23:7 tells us *"As a man thinks in his heart, so is he."* Our thoughts become our words, our words become our actions, and our actions become our habits.

Sometimes, I find myself feeling troubled or in a funk for no apparent reason. It's at those times I realize I need to take a step back and consider what I've been thinking about. More often than not, I realize my thoughts have been spiraling downward, throwing me off balance.

That's why it's so important to focus on thoughts that are true, honorable, right, pure, lovely, and of good report. Philippians 4:8 says, *"Finally, brothers and sisters, whatever is true, whatever is noble, whatever is right, whatever is pure, whatever is lovely, whatever is admirable - if anything is excellent or praiseworthy - think about such things. And the God of peace will be with you."*

Every time I read this verse, it acts like a bright light, guiding me towards a peaceful and purposeful life path. And when I'm on that path, I'm able to be a greater light to everyone I come in contact with.

REFLECTION

What negative thoughts do you tend to dwell on?

_____

_____

_____

_____

_____

_____

_____

Is there a scripture that can help you combat your negative thoughts?

_____

_____

_____

_____

_____

_____

You will keep in perfect peace those whose minds are steadfast, because they trust in you.

ISAIAH 26:3

DAY SEVENTEEN

The Sliver

IT WAS ONE of those lovely summer days. The sun was shining, the birds were singing, and my grandsons were out playing hide and seek, chasing the dogs, and playing in the garden as the adults were weeding. It was a joyful lighthearted day until my grandson, Ethan, screamed in a high-pitched voice.

Running to his father, Ethan showed his father how he had gotten a sliver in his hand from playing in a wooded area. After his dad, Ryan, comforted him, he told him the only way to get rid of the pain was to pull it out with a pair of tweezers.

"No, daddy, please don't do that. It would hurt too much," he said with tears streaming down his face.

Ryan calmly told Ethan he could keep the sliver in there, but it would only continue to hurt, or he could pull it out and have pain, but it would eventually get much better.

Ethan sadly looked into his father's eyes and said, "Dad isn't there any other way we could do it?" Ryan, being the wonderful father he is, gently told him that this was the only way, but he could be there hugging and holding him the whole time. Ethan finally agreed to have him do it, and even though it was very painful, he said it felt much better after it was removed.

What a fantastic comparison to God's healing work in our lives. We all have those deep slivers that God wants to remove, but we act like Ethan. "God, isn't there any other way?" When God shows us the slivers that are embedded in our souls, we try running and resisting Him. We don't want to go through the deep pain of removing our hurts, disappointments, and deep wounds that have caused our hearts to shrivel up. We would rather live with chronic pain instead of a short time of intense pain that we know would bring healing, wholeness, and a deeper walk with the Lord. He has our ultimate good in mind when He lovingly wants to remove these slivers from our hearts. Our fears keep us from trusting that God has our best interest in mind.

The beauty of this story ended when my daughter Valerie put ointment and a band-aid on Ethan's wound. Isn't that just like the Holy Spirit, who provides comfort and encouragement as we go through this transformation process?

What about you? Are you living with chronic pain because you're too afraid to allow the Lord to remove the painful slivers in your life? I pray you will be able to see beyond the pain into the deep healing that will come into your life.

REFLECTION

Are there any "slivers" in your life holding you back?

_____
_____
_____
_____
_____
_____

Write a prayer giving those "slivers" over to God:

_____
_____
_____
_____
_____
_____
_____
_____

For momentary light affliction is producing an eternal weight of glory far beyond all comparison.

I CORINTHIANS 4:7

DAY EIGHTEEN

The Father's Love

EPHESIANS 1:18 SAYS, *"I pray that the eyes of your heart may be enlightened so that you may know what is the hope of His calling, what are the riches of the Glory of His inheritance in the saints."* What is the surpassing power toward us who believe?

Do you ever feel there is so much more to life as a son or daughter of the King of Glory? Have you ever wished to truly live out the glorious life God created for you?

As I reflect on this glorious inheritance, I am reminded of a homeless young man. During the day, he wanders the streets, asking for handouts and begging for food. During the cold, lonely nights, he spends his nights huddling in a storefront corner. He is haunted by thoughts of what has become of his life. He questions himself unceasingly: *"Where did I go wrong?" What wrong choice have I made that brought me to this place of homelessness and hopelessness? Why did I leave the beauty and love of my home?"*

You see, this man's Father is a King, a loving Father whose heart breaks when He thinks about the life His son is living. He longs to embrace him and welcome him home to His palace, where He can pour out His Love and shelter him from the storms of life. He wants him to fully experience the rich and fulfilling life He has for him this whole time.

Our lives may not be that extreme, but the truth be told, we are all homeless in our own way, lost in our thoughts. We can't find our way back home until we accept we are lost and ask the Heavenly Father to guide us on the right path.

We have been left out in the cold for many reasons, but I believe the biggest reason is we have an enemy of our soul. He sets us on the way back home and detours us with all his deceptions and counterfeits. He knows and fears what we will become when we receive Our Father's love and live out what our true inheritance is.

How about you? Are you living fully and experiencing that abundant life that God has created for you, or are you sitting in a cold lonely place, afraid to reach out for our Father's love and provisions? I hope the eyes of your heart will be enlightened to all He has for you.

REFLECTION

What's holding you back from experiencing an abundant life?

_____

_____

_____

_____

_____

What steps can you take today to open your heart to your heavenly Father's love?

_____

_____

_____

_____

_____

_____

_____

_____

The thief comes to steal kill and destroy, I come that they may have life, and that they have it more abundantly.

JOHN 10:10

DAY NINETEEN

The Race

IN OUR LIVES, we often face challenges and what I like to refer to as 'Goliaths'. These challenges can seem insurmountable and overwhelming, making us feel like we can't possibly overcome them. That may be how Jehoshaphat felt when he was fighting against his adversaries. He was weary and felt like the battle against him was quite overwhelming.

But then the Lord showed up through the prayer of Jahziel. He said, *"Do not be dismayed because of this great multitude, for the battle is not yours but God's. You need not fight in this battle, station yourselves, stand firm and see the salvation of the Lord on your behalf."* (2 Chronicles 15 and 2 Chronicles 20:17)

I enjoy running 5k races because they challenge and fulfill me. But sometimes when I'm running, I feel overwhelmed by the race ahead of me. I start to focus on the other runners who are more experienced, and before I know it, negative thoughts and feelings start to creep in. It's like a battlefield in my mind, and I feel defeated before I even start the race.

So I decided to start training 4-5 days a week, running 4 miles each day. I slowly gained confidence with each practice. On the day of the race, I felt ready to do my best and not compare myself to the other athletes. And to my surprise, I took first place in that particular race. All glory to God!

I feel encouraged and comforted by what the Lord did for Jehoshaphat, and it reminds me that no matter what, God is fighting on my behalf. Take courage, my dear friend, as you let God help you overcome whatever obstacles stand in your way. Remember, if the Lord be for you, no one can be against you.

REFLECTION

What battle are you facing?

Have you ever experienced the Lord fighting on your behalf?

You will not need to fight in this battle. Stand firm and see the salvation of the Lord on your behalf.

2 CHRONICLES 20:17

DAY TWENTY

Fumes or Flames?

FUMES OR FLAMES? What is in your personal tank right now? Are you barely making it? Or are you going on full throttle by the power of the Holy Spirit?

Most of the time, we find ourselves in the first category, barely making it through the day because we are consumed with responsibilities, commitments, serving, and giving out until we run out of steam and stamina. In Matthew 11:28, Jesus says, *"Come to Me all you who are weary and heavy laden, and I will give you rest. Take my yoke upon you and learn from me, for I am gentle and humble in heart, and you shall find rest for your souls."* Wow, rest from all the burdens and save our weary souls? What an everlasting promise!

I personally experienced a time when I reached the bottom because I felt I could do everything without God, but I was wrong; my burden became more than I could handle. It was a tough time as life challenges overwhelmed me, and I felt burnt out beyond words. At this point, I surrendered all to God, praying fervently for a breakthrough.

One day, I heard the quiet, tiny voice of the Holy Spirit reach down, and I could feel the Holy Spirit breaking the chains and lifting the burdens that held me captive. I was filled with a newfound power by the Holy Spirit; I embraced God and acknowledged Him first above all things in my life.

There is abundant joy when we are free from any hindrance, captivity, or burden. I pray the same for you, that wherever you are, you will find rest, peace, and abundant joy in your soul so the flames of the Holy Spirit will bring you to your beautiful destination.

REFLECTION

What drains you the most?

Where do you go to refuel?

Come to me, all you who are weary and burdened,
and I will give you rest

MATTHEW 11:28

DAY TWENTY-ONE

Gifts from the Heart of Jesus

I WAS SO EXCITED as I wrapped the gifts for my loved ones one year for Christmas. I smiled at the thought of the joy each gift would bring them and how they would look around our tree. Suddenly, I had a vision of an even more beautiful tree surrounded by priceless gifts brought by the loving and generous heart of Jesus.

The first gift was a large golden one with a red bow. As I opened it, I read, "This is the gift of My unconditional love and the reason I came to earth. I have loved you with an everlasting love." This filled me with gratitude.

The second gift was glowing and contained the message, "The joy of the Lord is your strength. This gift of overflowing joy is so great that no circumstance can take it away from you." Tears of joy came to my eyes.

The third gift was wrapped in different shades of blue and had a golden bow. Inside, it read, "This is the gift of My peace that will surpass your greatest understanding." I felt a sense of awe and contentment as I read about this gift of peace.

The fourth gift was wrapped in brilliant yellow and had sunshine symbols on it. As I opened it, I read, "This is the gift of hope. My hope will never disappoint you because the love of the Father has been poured into you. If ever the world needed hope, it is now."

In the corner, I almost overlooked a small gift with the word "presence" written all over the wrapping. As I opened it, the words inside read, "This is the gift of My presence that will never leave you or forsake you. All these beautiful gifts will always bring you an awareness of My presence."

As I gazed at the tree and the gifts beneath it, I realized that it was these precious gifts that would bring warmth, tenderness, and meaning to every season. My heartfelt prayer for you is that these gifts will abound and overflow in your life today.

REFLECTION

What gift do you need the most in your life today?

_____
_____
_____
_____
_____
_____

Describe how this gift could bring more of God's presence in to your life:

_____
_____
_____
_____
_____
_____
_____

The fruit of the Spirit is love, joy, peace, patience kindness, generosity, faithfulness, gentleness, and self control.

GALATIANS 5:22-23

DAY TWENTY-TWO

Unbound and Free

AS WE LOOK FORWARD to celebrating the resurrection of Jesus, I was reflecting on Lazarus and how Jesus raised him from the dead. Before he was resurrected, Jesus told Lazarus to come forth as he was, bound hand and foot. In John 11:44, Jesus spoke to Lazarus after he died and said, *"Come forth"*, and he who died came forth bound hand and foot with wrappings and his face was covered with a cloth. Jesus said, *"Unbind him and let him go."*

As I was reflecting on this event, it struck me how so many of us have been bound and are wrapped in our guilt, shame, addictions, depression, emptiness, and loneliness. We hide in our coverings for fear that to come forth and be honest and vulnerable would be too painful. We fail to realize by "coming forth" into the light of Jesus' love and power, we will experience true freedom.

This was my life a few years ago. I was in the pit of darkness and depression. I was without hope and felt too ashamed to come forth and be released from the bondage that shackled me. There were many days when I felt overwhelmed, discouraged, and defeated. Fear and shame were holding me captive. Staying in this dark place had become safe, but I wasn't alive and felt dead inside.

In this broken place, the Lord gave me the courage to come forth and put my trust in Him. By God's grace and mercy, He released me from the shackles that held me captive for far too long. He empowered me with the courage to face these enemies of my soul. Was this journey easy? No. Soul work is never easy, but you come alive and live a wholehearted life in the end.

The resurrected Lazarus was a miracle that seemed impossible by all human standards. So it is with the enemies of our soul. It seems impossible that we will ever be free from them, yet that same power that raised Lazarus from the dead is available to us.

I encourage you to come forth with all that is holding you back. Allow the power and love of Jesus to resurrect you into a life of freedom and joy. You will soar to greater heights you never dreamt possible.

REFLECTION

In what ways are you bound?

_____
_____
_____
_____
_____
_____
_____
_____

What would your life look like if you were unbound and free?

_____
_____
_____
_____
_____
_____
_____
_____

If the Son shall make you free, you shall be free indeed.

JOHN 8:36

DAY TWENTY-THREE

Trusting and Waiting

WAS THERE EVER a time when your heart was yearning for an answer to prayer? When all you hear from God is "Trust and Wait?" The Scripture in Proverbs 3:5 brings this to light when Solomon says, *"Trust in the Lord with all your heart and do not lean on your own understanding."*

There was a time when my trust and patience were tested. My early years of marriage were challenging. Too often, we were at odds with each other, and it seemed like conflict resolution was impossible. It had to do with the fact that Randy and I were raised very differently. He came from a very stoic German background and talking about emotions was not acceptable. I, on the other hand, was raised where emotions were expressed daily, sometimes to an extreme when it caused hurt feelings. My family didn't keep much inside. So our communication styles were coming from extreme opposites.

Trust and wait. In the moment of trials and tribulations, those words seem difficult to receive, but by God's Grace, I was able to do that. The Scripture that sustained me was Isaiah 40:31, which says, *"Those who wait for the Lord will gain new strength. They will mount up with wings like eagles."* Oh, how I longed to rise above all the turmoil that was in my heart and be like the eagle that soars.

Just as spring follows winter, so it was with my marriage. The Lord brought healing and restoration beyond what my deepest prayers asked for. Was trusting easy? Not at all, but when I chose to let go and trust in God's perfect timing, He so faithfully answered my prayer. My husband and I now openly and honestly share our feelings and thoughts. We have a deeper level of communicating than I thought was ever possible. The Lord gave me strength as I waited on Him and a peace that surpassed my own understanding. *(Philippians 4:7)*

So, I encourage you in whatever you are waiting for, whether it's healing in your marriage, fulfillment of a promise the Lord gave you, the ability to let go and be able to forgive someone that hurt you, or anything else that you are hoping to see come to pass, to know that His timing is always perfect and He will fulfill the desires of your heart. Psalm 37:4, *"Delight yourself in the Lord and He will give you the desires of your heart."*

REFLECTION

What are you waiting to see come to pass in your life?

_____
_____
_____
_____
_____
_____
_____

Do you have a vision for what the Lord is going to do after you trust and wait?

_____
_____
_____
_____
_____
_____

Trust in the Lord with all your heart and do not lean on your own understanding.

PROVERBS 3:5

DAY TWENTY-FOUR

Glory: Fully Alive

AS I REFLECT ON THE GLORY of Christ's resurrection, my heart overflows with joy over the power of transformation that can take place in our lives. The beauty of Christ's death and resurrection is the way He enables and empowers us to become all He created us to be through His life-giving Spirit.

I love St. Irenaeus's quote, "The glory of God is a man fully alive." We are truly fully alive and reflect God's Glory when we allow Him to express Himself through our unique character.

One night while I was praying, I felt the Lord saying, "Allow Me to be who I am through you." The words kept ringing in my soul, and as I meditated, I realized I was not true to who God made me to be. I was going in different directions, trying to be and do things that weren't working. How could God use me if I wasn't living an authentic life and allowing Him to express Himself through my uniqueness?

Living our lives according to God's will is the only true way we can impact those around us, making the world a better place. When I look around, I see the amazing ways God expresses Himself through nature. An elephant isn't supposed to run like a cheetah; a dog is not meant to purr like a kitten; a sunflower is not meant to be fragrant like the lilac bush. If one is an introvert, he doesn't have to be the life of the party; if God created me to express myself through music, I shouldn't be behind a desk, crunching numbers.

These examples brought me Divine Relief and a

peace I hadn't experienced in a long time. I was *free* to be me, allowing me the ability to express who He made me to be without restraints or comparisons.

How about you? Are you celebrating the unique person God has created you to be? Or have you lost vision of who you are and fallen into the trap of trying to be someone else? Allowing God to be who He is through us is one of the most freeing and exhilarating experiences we have as we journey through this life.

I pray, as you celebrate the power of Christ's resurrection, He will grant you, according to the riches of His Glory, to be strengthened with Power through His Spirit so you will soar to new heights and experience the fullness of all He has prepared you for.

But now O Lord thou art our Father, we are the clay and Thou art the Potter, and all of us are the work of Your Hand.

ISAIAH 64:8

REFLECTION

What makes you feel fully alive?

_____
_____
_____
_____
_____
_____
_____

What gifts has God given you? And are you using them?

_____
_____
_____
_____
_____
_____
_____

Now there are varieties of gifts, but the same Spirit.
And there are varieties of ministries, and the same Lord.
There are varieties of effects, but the same God who
works all things in all persons.

1 CORINTHIANS 12:4-6

DAY TWENTY-FIVE

Victim or Victor

VICTIM OR VICTOR? These two words caught my attention as I read an inspiring book on overcoming. All too often, we think about our past and get stuck in the prison of thinking, *"I will never get out of this rut and all the bad things that are happening to me will never stop."* These thoughts defeat us before we even start, and before you know it, it becomes a self-fulfilling prophecy. You can't expect to be a victor if you're living with a victim mentality. It can become an identity if we continue in this pattern of thinking. Don't let your past define who you are; instead, use it as fuel to start a fresh beginning with right thinking and God's truth.

In Romans 8:37, Paul writes, *"We are more than conquerors through Him who loved us."* The power that comes from that truth is transforming. It changes us. In John 16:33, Jesus confirms what Paul was telling us. *"I have overcome the world. I have told you all this so that you may have peace in me. Here on earth, you will have many trials and sorrows,* **but take heart, I have overcome the world."**

In your own strength, you can't do it, but with the help of His Holy Spirit, you can experience new beginnings and be set free from the prison of a victim mentality. It's time to put the baggage behind you and experience a newfound freedom and victory. In 2 Corinthians 5:14-21, we read, *"Therefore, if any man is in Christ, he is a new creation, old things have passed away,* **behold all things become new.**"

Whatever your past is, you no longer have to let it define you. Our greatest blessings are contained in our greatest hardships. I pray you will see that Jesus is the key to setting you free.

REFLECTION

What does a victor look like to you?

Do you have any baggage from the past keeping you from living as a victor?

*One thing I do: forgetting what lies behind
and reaching forward for what is ahead. I press on toward
the goal to win the prize for which God has called me
heavenward in Christ Jesus.*

MATTHEW 11:28

DAY TWENTY-SIX

Getting Unstuck

OVER THE YEARS, I have consistently exercised, not because I like it, but I love the feeling of exhilaration I get afterward. Even good routines like this have the entrapment of reaching plateaus, and we're not seeing the results we're working so hard for.

So often, I have hit these plateaus where I am very comfortable in what I'm doing, but there is no evidence of building muscle, losing weight, or getting toned. I need to challenge myself by using heavier weights, raising the incline, and pushing myself even harder. Easy, no. Results, yes.

This whole realization got me thinking about our own personal challenges and trials we face.

Everything in us wants to run and resist going through this test of our perseverance. James 1:12 says, *"Blessed is the man who perseveres under trials or (challenges) for once he has been approved he will receive the crown of life which the Lord has promised to those who love Him."*

In other words, growing our spiritual muscles comes through persevering and embracing our difficult time, knowing we will grow in character and receive the crown of life Christ promised us.

So go ahead, get those spiritual muscles built up so you will be prepared to face and overcome the challenges that come your way. 1 Peter 1:6, *"In this you greatly rejoice, even though now for a little while, if necessary, you have been distressed by various trials. That the proof of your faith, being more precious than gold which is perishable, even though tested by fire, may result in praise, glory, and honor at the revelation of Jesus Christ."*

REFLECTION

How can you challenge yourself to become unstuck?

What spiritual muscles will help you persevere?

All discipline for the moment seems not to be joyful, but sorrowful, yet to those who have been trained by it afterward it yields the peaceful fruit of righteousness.

HEBREWS 12:11

DAY TWENTY-SEVEN

Are You Blooming?

I LOVE TO WATCH my African violets flourish. I tend to them like a mother would her child - ensuring they receive the right amount of sunlight, proper drainage, and regular watering and fertilization. One day, as I was performing my caretaking duties, I noticed the once prolific violets were shedding their flowers and no new buds were appearing.

Upon closer examination, I was surprised to discover the violet had become pot-bound and split into three separate plants. These new plants were waiting to be transplanted so they could grow and flourish as three separate, individual plants.

This realization led me to reflect on my own life and ask myself some heartfelt questions. *Am I still blooming? Is my life flourishing? Has God done a deeper work in me that has made me "pot-bound"? Do I need to step out of my comfort zone in order to be used in even greater ways?* These questions made me uncomfortable, but deep down, I knew it was time to step out of my comfort zone and move in rhythm with the Holy Spirit's direction.

Just like the violets, I know when I step out of my comfort zone and allow myself to be transplanted, I may initially go through a period of shock. It can be cozy staying in our comfort zones, but we must remember it's not always best for us to stay there.

There comes a time in our journey when we must pay attention and strive for greater depths and heights, so the beauty of our blooms can bring beauty to the lives of others. Fear of the unknown is often what holds us back, and the enemy wants us to stay put so we do not make a difference in the world.

Even though it may feel uncomfortable, we must step out in faith, knowing the Lord will equip and enable us to fulfill our deeper purpose. The will of God will never take us where His grace cannot keep us.

What is holding you back? Are you feeling stuck and sensing a stirring in your heart for something greater than what you are currently experiencing? I encourage you to step out in faith, trusting the Lord will bring a greater depth of fulfillment and joy to your life than you ever imagined.

REFLECTION

Is there a stirring in your heart to start blooming?

_____

_____

_____

_____

_____

_____

_____

What is one thing you can do to get out of your comfort zone?

_____

_____

_____

_____

_____

_____

_____

Now to Him who is able to do immeasurably more than all we ask or imagine, according to his power that is at work within us, to him be glory in the church and in Christ Jesus throughout all generations, for ever and ever! Amen.

EPHESIANS 3:20

DAY TWENTY-EIGHT

Let the Rains Come

IT WAS ONE OF THE rainiest summers I could remember. The sun didn't visit us too often and the skies remained overcast. At the same time, I was going through a personal season of ongoing rain. Everything felt as gloomy as the sky above me. I didn't understand why I would cry at the drop of a hat.

I related to David when he said in Psalm 42:3, "My tears have been my food day and night, while they say to me all day long, 'Where are you, God?'"

The rains finally subsided, and I thought it would be a good time to do some gardening. I had a raised bed filled with an array of beautiful flowers of all colors, shapes, and sizes. As I knelt down to check the status of my garden, I noticed that the weeds were trying to take over the flowers. I decided it was time to get busy with this overwhelming task of weed picking.

Once I started, I was quite taken aback by the ease in which the weeds uprooted themselves. I was actually enjoying this activity when a gentle and loving thought came to my mind, "Your season of tears is allowing me to uproot the weeds that have crowded around your heart. Without the tears, I could never get to the roots." *Wow*, I thought to myself.

The worries, doubt, self-occupation, and countless other "weeds" were all displayed before me. I realized that unless I allowed the Holy Spirit to uproot these weeds, the beauty of my flowers (fruit of the spirit) would be overtaken by the weeds of my flesh. Weeding had never been more rewarding that when I realized the purpose of the process!

What about you? Are you in a season of rain, and the weeds are trying to overtake the beauty of your heart and soul? Proverbs 4:23, *"Watch over your heart with all diligence for from it flow the springs of life."*

Today I pray God's grace and strength will bless you abundantly as you pull the weeds from your life and give yourself room to bloom.

REFLECTION

In what ways have you been experiencing a personal "season of rain" in your life?

_____
_____
_____
_____
_____
_____

How can you allow the Holy Spirit to uproot the weeds in your life?

_____
_____
_____
_____
_____
_____

To grant those who mourn in Zion, Giving them a garland instead of ashes, The oil of gladness instead of mourning, The mantle of praise instead of a spirit of fainting. So they will be called oaks of righteousness, The planting of the LORD, that He may be glorified.

ISAIAH 61:3

DAY TWENTY-NINE

How is Your Soul?

"HOW ARE YOU?" That's a common courteous question we often ask people. We get many different answers, most of which are superficial. I'm fine, busy, and tired, to name a few.

A question I've been reflecting on lately is, "How is your soul?" Now, that's a question that makes most of us squirm and get a little bit uncomfortable. One may think, *"That's too deep, or I'm not sure I want to answer that for fear I may have to admit what's really going on."*

I wonder, if we were brutally honest, would we answer, "My soul is malnourished." Now, that's a powerful response and yet is probably more true for most of us than we would like to admit. Just like our bodies become malnourished from lack of food, water, and sleep, our souls suffer from lack of quiet, rest, reflection, meditation, prayer, and so much more.

John Eldredge talks about the beauty of a "soul sabbath." Sabbath reconnects you to the God who loves you and allows you time to linger with Him unhurried. It also reconnects you with your own soul and allows you to think about stuff you normally don't get to think of.

Our soul is what makes us come alive. It helps us see and experience all the beauty that surrounds us. It enables us to connect on a deeper level with those we love and cherish and gives us a heightened awareness of the abundance that is in our life.

How do we diagnose a malnourished soul? Just like our bodies give us signs and symptoms, so our souls tell us by feelings of burnout, lack of real connection to people, feelings of just going through the motions of living, and most importantly, feeling a disconnect from God. These are just a few of the telltale signs alerting us to the fact all is not well.

So, what do we do? First, stop and put the pause button on our lives. As we quiet our souls long enough, we need to reflect and reevaluate what is draining the life out of our souls. Too many hours at work, stress from trying to keep your head above water, busyness, depression, anxiety, and no alone time. These may be just a few of the reasons.

Just as a doctor doesn't give you a diagnosis without giving you a treatment plan, so it is with God. He calls us to deeper waters where we can find rest for our weary souls. In Matthew 11:28 Jesus says, *"Come unto me all you who are weary and heavy laden and I will give you rest."*

When we quiet our souls and slow down our pace, we will find a peace that surpasses our own understanding. Philippians 4:7, *"And the peace of*

God which surpasses all comprehension shall guard your hearts and minds." We will also experience a joy that overflows and a strength that is beyond our own.

What is holding you back from taking time to restore your soul? Jesus said, *"What shall a man profit if he gains the world but loses his soul?" (Matthew 16:26)* I encourage you to nourish yourself with soul food that will refresh, restore, renew, and revive you. The Lord will reveal what you need and will also give you the strength to make the changes necessary so your soul is restored. May you find times of refreshing from His loving heart to yours.

REFLECTION

How would you answer the question "How is your soul?"

_____
_____
_____
_____
_____
_____

What type of soul food do you need today?

_____
_____
_____
_____
_____
_____

Do not be grieved, for the joy of the Lord is your strength.

NEHEMIAH 8:10

DAY THIRTY

Take Time to Smell the Roses

TODAY, AS I WAS having my morning coffee, I looked out the window and saw the beautiful sunrise. As I looked out another window, I saw a hummingbird sipping nectar from a flower. It reminded me of the expression "Take time to smell the roses."

We often find ourselves on the fast track of life, preoccupied and overwhelmed by everything that competes for our attention and prevents us from seeing and experiencing the beauty of nature that surround us. How often do we overlook the treasures of glory standing right in front of us?

Our souls were created to behold and experience the glory and beauty the Lord has created for us. A delicate flower, the rising and setting of the sun, snow-capped mountains, a baby's giggle, the comfort of connecting with friends and family - the list goes on and on. These are all things which awaken our weary souls and minds.

I like to think of these things as 'soul pleasures'. They are gifts that the Lord has given us to renew, refresh, and restore us, so we are fortified to live the abundant life He has created for us. Psalm 103:5 says, *"He satisfies our life with good things so that our youth is renewed like the eagle."* To behold and take in these gifts is a beautiful form of worship.

May the Lord bless you as you take time to enjoy the beauty of His creation and may it be a reminder of His goodness and love for you.

REFLECTION

How can you make a habit of taking time to "smell the roses" and notice the beauty in your everyday life?

_____

_____

_____

_____

_____

_____

In what ways do you think noticing and appreciating the beauty of nature can bring you closer to God?

_____

_____

_____

_____

_____

_____

The heavens declare the glory of God, and the sky above proclaims his handiwork.

PSALM 19:1

DAY THIRTY-ONE

Listen to Your Inner GPS

WHEN I WAS DRIVING home one day, I needed to use my GPS to find my way back. As I was following the directions, it guided me to go down a certain street that was unfamiliar to me. I didn't follow the directions and went the way I thought was right. I ended up going considerably out of my way. What should have been a 15-minute drive ended up being over 30 minutes.

I suppose you might know where I'm going with this one. So often we hear the Lord telling us to go in a certain direction, but decide to change course and go another way. We believe we know the way and we choose to go in another direction. We end up wasting time and effort and become frustrated. Psalm 32:8 tells us, *"He will instruct and teach you the way to go: He will counsel you with His eye upon you."*

So many times we end up going in circles until we realize we need to listen to our inner GPS (God's Protective Spirit). Even if it feels unfamiliar or uncomfortable, His direction for our life brings us to beautiful and amazing places. It's where we find joy, peace and fulfillment.

We need to ask ourselves what causes us to go our own way. Is it fear of the unknown? Are we tuning God out or just plain stubborn? I believe, once we can identify the root cause, we can trust He only has the best in mind for us.

We can plan, but God's GPS will direct us. My hope and prayer for you is that, in the coming days you will listen to your inner GPS and arrive at the perfect destination He has prepared for you.

REFLECTION

Have you ever found yourself going in a different direction than your inner GPS? (God's Protective Spirit)

_____
_____
_____
_____
_____
_____
_____

What lessons did you learn from that experience?

_____
_____
_____
_____
_____
_____
_____

*The mind of the man plans his way,
but the Lord will direct his steps.*

PROVERBS 3:9

Acknowledgments

FIRST AND FOREMOST, I dedicate this book to my Lord and Savior, Jesus Christ. He brought daily inspirations and analogies to my mind and heart. Through His Spirit, He equipped me to persevere through each obstacle and setback I experienced. Without Him at my side, this devotional would not be in your hands.

To my faithful, loving renaissance husband, Randy, you were undoubtedly the wind beneath my wings throughout this process. You gave me vision when I was short-sighted and encouragement when I was weary. You patiently and lovingly read and reread each of my entries and provided feedback and advice on how I could bring more life into each of my writings. You were at my side through all my ups and downs and everything in between. I am forever grateful to you.

To my gentle giant daughter, Valerie. You were a force to be reckoned with when you kept telling me I needed to share my story. You helped me give birth to this devotional, and I am deeply grateful you never gave up on me. When self-doubt tried to take over, you gently reminded me of the gift God had given me and how important it was to use it. When I was ready to give up, you somehow knew what I needed to hear to keep going. You played a vital role in my journey and helped me bring this to fruition.

To my tenacious and fearless daughter Summer. You demonstrated to me through your words and example what it is to be a warrior. No matter how big the challenge, you showed me the power within each of us. And when we tap into that power, anything is possible. Thank you for believing in me and showing me that courage and perseverance do make dreams come true.

To my dear and loving sisters, Karen, Anne Marie, and Nettie. Each of you played an incredible part in making my dream a reality. You cheered me on

ACKNOWLEDGMENTS

throughout this whole process. You would read my writings and always give me wonderful feedback. My heart is so grateful the Lord gave me the gift of your friendship and sisterhood.

To my faithful and loyal brother Jerry. You were my prayer warrior throughout the months I labored in my writings. Your prayers are what sustained and fortified me. You showed me what the power of prayer can do. Thank you so very much.

To my dedicated editor Abigail Wolfer. Your ability to bring out the best in my writing with your edits and suggestions was so very helpful. I am so very grateful for the time and dedication you gave to make my devotional the best it could be. I hope we can continue to work together with any future books I may write.

To my creative and helpful designer/formatter, Meg Delagrange-Belfon. Like a puzzle, your role in all you contributed made everything fit together beautifully. Your ideas, creative input, and encouragement helped me to believe this was all possible. Thank you so much for your dedication and availability to me.

To my loving and dear friends, that are too many to name, I am so grateful for all of the support and encouragement you gave to me. The words each of you spoke to me were like the wind in my sails that brought me to my destination.

Meet the Author

JUDY MAID IS a gifted author and psychiatric nurse who has dedicated her life to helping others find hope and inspiration. Her book, **Weaving Threads of Gold**, is a 31-day devotional that draws on her personal experiences and professional knowledge to offer readers a powerful and uplifting message.

A native of Chicago, Judy has called Colorado home for the past 28 years, where she lives with her husband Randy and their two daughters. With

45 years of marriage under her belt, she has a deep understanding of the importance of family and relationships.

Judy is also a devout believer who has been on her spiritual journey for over 50 years. She is dedicated to her walk with the Lord and is always looking for ways to discover hope in unexpected places. As a psychiatric nurse for over 23 years, Judy has helped countless individuals find hope and healing in their lives, and her passion for helping others is evident in her work and writing.

In her free time, Judy enjoys reading, running 5k races, writing, and playing Pickleball. Her diverse interests and experiences give her a unique perspective on the human experience, which she shares in her writing, offering readers a message of hope, healing, and inspiration.

CONNECT WITH *Judy*

✉ JUDYMAID@YAHOO.COM

★★★★★

I have had the privilege of working with Judy and have experienced significant breakthroughs because of it! Through our time together I have had so much clarity and am now working within my passions and life calling.

SHARON LAMZ

★★★★★

Judy is an excellent example of what a Life Coach should be. Judy is approachable, personable, friendly and very helpful. She is enthusiastic, empathetic with a great sense of humor. With all of these great qualities Judy will exceed any and all expectations.

ANNE MARIE MAGNETTA

★★★★★

I have known Judy for sixty years and counting. Judy is a very compassionate individual who has great empathy for others. One of her greatest qualities is listening to others and seeing where they are coming from and always giving support to others.

EILEEN MARLOWE

★★★★★

Judy has been instrumental in helping me find my passion and gave me the courage to go for it. I am now living a more joy filled life because of her investment in me. I highly recommend meeting with her!

LYNN

WORK WITH *Judy*

Do you sense there's more to life than what you've experienced so far? Are you held back by circumstances, old habits, or confusion? Are you ready to step into the future God has designed you for? As a Christian Certified Life Coach, Judy helps people move from "the rut" and into a life they've courageously crafted for themselves. It's time to take action and pursue the life you're meant to live.

WWW.COACHINGYOURTRUEYOU.COM

www.ingramcontent.com/pod-product-compliance
Lightning Source LLC
Chambersburg PA
CBHW021433060526
44119CB00107B/455/J